GERMAN FIGHTERS OVER ENGLAND

The Messerschmitt Bf 109 saw service throughout the war and in every theatre; starting its life with the Luftwaffe as a comparatively simple fighter and gradually being developed beyond all recognition. These examples, photographed just prior to the outbreak of war in 1939, are C models, and even at this time carry a variety of markings, some of which are contrary to laid down policy; thus setting the scene which still causes controversy 40 years later! (379/15/18).

BRYAN PHILPOTT

GERMAN FIGHTERS OVER ENGLAND

WORLD WAR 2 PHOTO ALBUM NUMBER 10

A selection of German wartime photographs
from the Bundesarchiv, Koblenz

PSL Patrick Stephens, Cambridge

First published in 1979

British Library Cataloguing in Publication Data

German fighters over England. – (World War 2 photo
   albums; 10).
   1. World War, 1939–1945 – Aerial operations, German
   – Pictorial works   2. Britain, Battle of, 1940 –
   Pictorial works   3. Fighter planes – History –
   Pictorial works
   I. Philpott, Bryan   II. Series
   940.54'21   D787

   ISBN 0 85059 355 7 (casebound)
   ISBN 0 85059 356 5 (softbound)

Photoset in 10pt Plantin Roman. Printed in Great
Britain on 100 gsm Pedigree coated cartridge and
bound by The Garden City Press Limited,
Letchworth, Hertfordshire, SG6 1JS, for the
publishers, Patrick Stephens Limited, Bar Hill,
Cambridge, CB3 8EL

CONTENTS

Acknowledgement
The author and publisher would like to express their sincere thanks to Frau Marianne Loenartz of the Bundesarchiv for her assistance, without which this book would have been impossible.

Main Luftwaffe fighter bases in France and Belgium August 1940, also demarcation of RAF Groups

LUFTFLOTTE 5
(NORWAY)

NO 12 GROUP

Norwich

North Weald
Hornchurch
Croydon
Kenley
Biggin Hill

NO 11 GROUP

NO 10 GROUP

Exeter

St Eval

Plymouth

Wissant
St Omer
Etaples
Montreuil
Crécy-en-Ponthieu
Abbeville
Arques
Barley Amiens

LUFTFLOTTE 2

Le Havre

Caudron
Caen
Guyancourt
Beaumont-le-Roger

Alençon

LUFTFLOTTE 3

Laval
Le Mans
Étampes

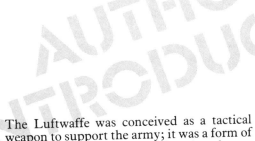

The Luftwaffe was conceived as a tactical weapon to support the army; it was a form of aerial artillery which laid before the advancing infantry a carpet of devastation over which they could advance with a degree of impunity.

Medium twin-engined bombers and single-engined dive-bombers formed the strike element, operating in air space controlled by fighter squadrons which cleared the way by destroying any opposing air forces. This, at least, was the theory and, during the advance through Poland, the Low Countries and France, it proved to be sound. German fighters met very little serious interference from the obsolete aircraft and tactics of those who tried to stop them, and the bombers were able to carry out their Blitzkrieg with only minor losses. In France the story was not entirely the same because the RAF was able to provide stronger resistance, albeit with Hurricanes which were inferior to the Bf 109Es. The methods used by the British were a legacy from the massed air battles of World War 1. The Luftwaffe, however, had been able to discard old tactics in favour of new and effective ones learned and perfected in the skies of Spain. None the less, the quality of training, airmanship and ruggedness of the RAF pilots and their equipment was enough to make some Luftwaffe fighter pilots realise that any task they were set over England would not be as easy as it had been in Poland and the Low Countries.

The absence of a long-range strategic bomber was to cost the Germans dearly – some argue it cost them total victory – and it is a little hard to understand why the importance of such a weapon was not appreciated, especially as the Imperial German Air Force had pioneered its use against England in World War 1.

When the new Luftwaffe was revealed to a disbelieving world in March 1935, it was the best equipped air force in the world, a position it maintained until 1940 when events began to disclose its inherent weaknesses. The Munich agreement of 1938 gave Britain valuable breathing space for, if she had gone to war then, RAF Fighter Command could only have matched the modern monoplane fighters of the Luftwaffe with obsolescent biplanes and the outcome would have been far different. As it was, in the two years from Munich to the intrusion into British air space of enemy fighters, production of modern eight-gun monoplane fighters had progressed at a feverish pace and by the time the Battle of Britain started, Fighter Command strength, in terms of modern equipment, was almost at parity with that of the Luftwaffe. In an endeavour to add colour to the events of 1940, many writers and some historians have been guilty of perpetuating the popular myth of an outnumbered core of tired pilots fighting against a far superior enemy. Although not detracting from the bravery and determination of the 'few', the facts are that the fighter strength of the RAF was almost identical to that of the Luftwaffe's Jagdgruppen, and there were greater numbers of aircraft in reserve. The popular misconception arises because quite often the *total* strength of the Luftwaffe, without regard to those engaged on other fronts or in reserve, is quoted as opposing Fighter Command only or, in some cases where the writer has been a little more objective, he has fallen into the trap of quoting the totals of bombers and fighters ranged against the RAF. In essence the outcome of the battle depended on the ability of the Luftwaffe fighter pilots to clear the skies of British fighters thus giving their bombers freedom of operation. In the end they failed because they were restricted in their operational combat time over England, hampered by a directive which tied them to protecting bomber formations, unsettled by a change in tactics which involved them in attacking RAF airfields rather than strategic targets and, finally, the growing strength of Fighter Command towards the end of the summer of 1940 proved to be a great obstacle.

The Luftwaffe was not trained or equipped to fight a long strategic battle as it was an air force primarily to be used for co-operation with land forces. When it encountered what has been described as the best defensive fighter of the war, the Spitfire, ably supported by the inferior but rugged

Hurricane, it was defeated. Apart from the restriction previously mentioned, the Jagdgruppen were at a disadvantage in that they were fighting over hostile territory where to be shot down meant certain capture, and they had no system to combat the extremely effective radar control of the British fighter squadrons. One major advantage they had in the early days of aerial combat over the British Isles was that they no longer used the outdated formation tactics evolved from the days of World War 1. Experience in the Spanish Civil War was quickly passed to all new fighter pilots through the training schools, and the soundness of the methods used is reflected in their adoption by all air forces by the time hostilities ceased.

The basic Luftwaffe unit was the Rotte which was a pair of fighters flying about 150 yards apart, each pilot searching inwards so that he covered his companion's blind spots. One of the pair would be the leader (Rottenführer) and the other his wing-man (Katchmarek), two such pairs formed a Schwarm which operated with one Rotte slightly ahead and to the side of the other; a good impression of the formation can be gained from looking at the finger-tips of an outstretched hand. When flying in Staffel strength three Schwaerme would fly in finger-four formation stepped up in line astern. In enemy air space where opposing fighters were likely to be encountered, high cruising speeds were maintained and, in the event of a large formation performing a turn without reducing speed, the outer aircraft were prevented from becoming stragglers by the simple expedient of a cross-over turn which enabled positions and direction to be altered without speed loss. Fighter pilots were taught to use the sun as an ally and gain height above their opponents before diving from it to hit them in one firing pass, the speed gained in such a dive could be used to regain height and repeat the manoeuvre.

Tactics like this, and a firm belief in their aircraft and equipment, was a vital part of Luftwaffe pilots' training, which up to the early days of World War 2 took just over two years to complete. Apart from the soundness of the basic design of the Bf 109, pilots also had first class personal equipment including a Mauser flare pistol which was attached to the life-jacket by a cord, a one-man dinghy fastened to the parachute harness, and flying gear which often left a certain amount of choice open to the individual. The kit could also include a one-piece flying overall or leather flight jacket worn over, or with, normal uniform. The Bf 109's cockpit was well protected by armour plating above the pilot's head and to either side of his body, as well as a 56 mm thick bullet-proof windscreen. A disadvantage was the rather cramped confines of the cockpit, especially for a tall man, and the surprisingly limited radio equipment which, almost unbelievably, could not be used for direct communication with bomber crews.

With new aircraft, replacement pilots, and the confidence brought by successful campaigns, the Jagdgruppen of Luftflotten 2 and 3 stood poised on their airfields in France and Belgium to carry the fight across the Channel to the waiting Royal Air Force.

Losses over the Dunkirk beach-head indicated to those Luftwaffe pilots involved that the fighters of the RAF would be an entirely different proposition to those engaged over France, especially the Spitfire which had taken a heavy toll of Ju 87s and their covering Bf 109s. But most of them were not unduly concerned, for they believed that the strength of the RAF was much lower than it was, and the much greater Luftwaffe bomber and fighter strengths would present too large a problem.

At this time the strength of Luftflotten 2 and 3 was 760 Bf 109Es and 220 Bf 110s, of which approximately 85 per cent were serviceable and ready for combat. It is helpful to understand the Luftwaffe chain of command which, to a degree, was cumbersome and in some cases led to individual Luftflotten commanders making serious errors of judgement. Each Luftflotte was virtually a self-contained air force which in turn was split into separate divisions – Fliegerdivisionen – which were sub-divided into specialist units each being roughly equivalent to an RAF Wing and known as Geschwadern. The function of a Geschwader was defined by its title, hence a Jagdgeschwader (JG) was a fighter unit, a Kampfgeschwader (KG) a bomber unit, a Nachtjagdgeschwader (NJG) a night fighter unit, and so on. The Geschwader had an approximate strength of 90 aircraft and was identified by a number and initials, for example, JG 2, KG 3, etc. The Geschwader was again divided into Gruppen which were numbered with Roman style figures. There were usually four Gruppen each of which was broken down into three Staffeln and a Stab (staff) flight. Each

9

Staffel was identified by Arabic numerals and comprised between ten and 12 aircraft, the Stab flight being separate and having four or five aircraft. The Staffel was therefore the smallest flying unit and very roughly approximated to an RAF squadron; it was commanded by a Staffelkapitan and had its own communications, vehicles and staff. Gruppen had their own identifying symbols, in the case of fighters carried behind the fuselage cross and, in twin-engined fighters and bombers, replaced by a code letter in the same position. Each Staffel had its own colour which in many cases was used to outline individual aircraft codes or Gruppe markings.

Every Geschwader operated within its own sector with its Gruppen dispersed at various airfields. It was not unusual for Gruppen to share an airfield or, on the other hand, to be widely dispersed across a large geographical area.

This rather over-simplified explanation should enable the reader to appreciate that a reference to I/JG 2 would indicate the first Gruppe of Jagdgeschwader 2, while 7/JG 2 would refer to the seventh Staffel of JG 2. The latter example could also be written 7/III/JG 2, but this method was rarely used as once the allocation of the Staffeln was known, it was simple to identify the Gruppe. I Gruppe comprised Staffeln 1, 2 and 3; II Gruppe 4, 5 and 6; III Gruppe 7, 8 and 9: and IV Gruppe 10, 11 and 12.

Luftflotte 2 was commanded by Generalfeldmarschall Albert Kesselring who had commanded Luftflotte 1 in Poland, and Luftflotte 3 by Generalfeldmarschall Hugo Sperrle whose guiding hand had looked after the Legion Kondor in Spain. Both men were immensely experienced army-trained officers who, by virtue of their very training, looked upon the Luftwaffe as an extension of the artillery to be used to smash a path for the army. The coming battles in England were to force them to change their views.

By July 1940, the planned invasion of England was about to enter its first phase with Göring briefing his three Luftflotten to attack the RAF by day and night, in the air and on the ground.

On July 12 RAF Fighter Command had on strength 670 fighters ready for combat, and a further 513 in reserve at maintenance units, so as far as fighters were concerned the opposing air forces were virtually equal. But equality cannot be judged on numbers alone,

many other factors must be considered. Important among these was radar, which had been perfected to a greater degree by the British than the German High Command appreciated, and was the key in getting the defending fighters into positions where they were most needed. Initially the Luftwaffe firmly believed that the RAF was mounting costly standing patrols which would help to weaken the defenders since such patrols are tiring and wearing on men and machines. As far as the aircraft were concerned, the Bf 109 was a nimble and very manoeuvrable aircraft armed with two 20 mm wing-mounted cannon and two 7·9 mm fuselage-mounted machine-guns, or a similar combination depending on the version concerned, which were far more devastating than the eight ·303 (7·7 mm) wing-mounted machine-guns of the Hurricane and Spitfire. Performance comparisons of the aircraft are misleading if taken out of context, so there is little point in making precise comparisons in a narrative such as this. However, it is acceptable to state that, in very general terms, the Hurricane was inferior in performance to the Bf 109, whereas the Spitfire was about equal, especially in the height band between 13,000 and 20,000 feet where most combats were fought during the summer of 1940. One big disadvantage the British fighters had to contend with was that, if they were pushed over into a dive, their engines would momentarily cut out as centrifugal force upset the float-operated carburettor, whereas the direct fuel injected motors of the Bf 109s were not affected by such manoeuvres.

So the scene was set for the Luftwaffe to start their allotted task of clearing the skies over the Channel and southern England, thus enabling the proposed invasion to proceed without any hindrance from the RAF. Initial skirmishes began in the Channel area when fighters harried convoys and bombers attacked ports and shipping. In some cases the bombers were escorted by fighters, in others the fighters simply flew Frei Jagd (Free Chase) patrols aimed at drawing the RAF into combat. These tactics succeeded to a degree and, in the first week of July, Fighter Command lost 18 fighters and 13 pilots. One of the earliest large-scale combats developed on the morning of July 10 when Bf 109s and Bf 110s from JG 3, 27, 51 and ZG 76 escorted bombers attacking the convoy code named Bread off North Foreland.

In many cases the Spitfire and Hurricane

squadrons which were scrambled to meet these early threats operated at a distinct disadvantage since they had no opportunity to gain height before the Bf 109s dived on them. With height and speed advantage, the Luftwaffe pilots held all the aces and the British fighters suffered accordingly. These early exchanges taught both sides a great deal and the RAF was soon to adopt the finger-four formation used by the Luftwaffe, but old methods die hard and even at the height of the battle on August 18 Hurricanes of No 501 Squadron were caught climbing in Vics of three by III/JG 26. Oberleutnant Gerhard Schoepfel dived his Bf 109 from the sun and immediately shot down the Hurricanes of Pilot Officers Bland and Kozlowski who were guarding the squadron's tail. The remaining Hurricanes, unaware that their weavers had gone, continued to climb and Schoepfel with his wing-man accounted for two more before the others realised what was happening. Only one of the pilots was killed, the other three parachuting to safety. This was one advantage which the RAF had over the Luftwaffe which lost all pilots shot down over England. At this time the German training squadrons could still produce pilots whereas, as far as the RAF was concerned, they were in very short supply. The Luftwaffe's biggest problem was the replacement of aircraft, as in 1940 their production rate was only about half of that of the British.

Throughout July and August the Luftwaffe Jagdgruppen had discovered to their cost that the RAF possessed more fighters than they had been led to believe, and they were flown by pilots whose tenacity and resolve to defend their homeland was such that the estimated numbers of fighters needed for escort was woefully underestimated. Another painful lesson was that the twin-engined Bf 110 was no match for the Hurricane or Spitfire – although it was not so greatly outclassed by the former – and it needed a fighter escort of its own or had to rely on a far-from-effective defensive circle.

As Göring became more and more frustrated at the failure of the Luftwaffe to carry out his promise to Hitler, activity by the bombers was increased and the fighters were tied to them in close escort. With a combat radius of action reaching only to London, and sufficient fuel to allow a maximum of 15 minutes combat over England, the Bf 109 pilots became more and more inhibited. From early July to the second week of August, the Jagdgruppen lost 106 Bf 109s and Bf 110s against a total of 148 British fighters, but among this total was a number of Defiants which had been decimated before being withdrawn from the battle, and some obsolete twin-engined Blenheims. This rate of attrition could be sustained by the Luftwaffe, but it was losing too many bombers without achieving the breakthroughs expected. A change of tactics came in mid-August when attention was turned to the radar installations along the coast, and RAF airfields. Considerable damage was caused and although losses on both sides were high, those of the Bf 110 Zerstörers were disastrous with 26 being accounted for on August 15, of which five came from the Norwegian based Luftflotte 5 I/ZG 76.

Göring made several changes to the command structure of the Jagdflieger during mid-August, introducing younger pilots with what he termed 'a more aggressive spirit' to command positions. But having done this, he was not then content to allow such men as Galland, Trautloft and Lutzlow to introduce their own form of independent fighter operations. If the attacks mounted against RAF installations had been allowed to continue with top priority and all other major air operations suspended, the Luftwaffe might well have achieved Göring's aims, but a switch to strategic targets in late August gave the RAF much-needed breathing space. There is no doubt that Fighter Command was almost at the end of its tether, and on August 31 it suffered its highest casualties of the period, when 25 Hurricanes and 12 Spitfires were shot down with the loss of 12 pilots killed and several hospitalised. In mid-August practically all the Bf 109s of Luftflotte 3 were transferred to the command of Luftflotte 2 and based on airfields around the Pas de Calais. This gave an overwhelming provision of escorts, but effective combat range was still the major problem; if the 300-litre (66 Imperial gallon) drop tank had been available two months before it was generally issued, the Jagdgruppen would have had a distinct advantage in combat radius. But all types of warfare are interspersed with ifs and buts and every commander has 100 per cent hindsight.

Diversionary attacks, feints and fighter sweeps aimed at catching the RAF on the ground, were all part of the Jagdgruppen effort throughout August. The fact they accounted for nearly 500 fighters lost or severely damaged is testimony to their success. But more serious as far as the defenders were concerned, was the loss of pilots who could not be replaced fast enough. In early September the point of attack was changed to the bombing of London, this coming as a direct reprisal for the RAF's activity over Berlin. This change played a major part in the recovery of Fighter Command, for their airfields were no longer attacked with the same intensity and as bomber sorties increased, straightforward fighter operations were curtailed. The Bf 109s and 110s were now firmly tied to the bombers and thus became less effective in their designed role. The tactics adopted by the RAF were to use Spitfires to try to intercept and engage the escort fighters and, while they were thus occupied, the Hurricanes moved in against the bombers. By introducing high-speed bombers such as the Ju 88, escorted by Bf 109s, the Luftwaffe hoped to reduce its loss rate, but this ploy did not meet with the total success hoped for and it became more and more apparent as September went on that the invasion could not take place.

The climax of the Battle of Britain, and the day which is regarded as being the one which finally brought defeat to the Luftwaffe, was Sunday September 15 1940. On this occasion the Germans mounted a series of sorties which gave the defending squadrons a trying time, but at the end of the day the Luftwaffe was a demoralised force having lost 60 aircraft of which 26 were fighters. Among those lost were Oberleutnant Reumschüssel, the Staffel Kapitan of 2/JG 3, Oberleutnant Jase, the Staffel Kapitan of 3/JG 53 and Leutnant Berthol, the Adjutant of Stab I/JG 52.

Sporadic activity continued into November during which time the use of fighter bombers became a regular feature of the Jagdgruppen. At this time the aircraft were modified versions of the Bf 109E adapted to carry a 550 lb (250 kg) bomb on a centre-rack. These aircraft often formed the fourth Gruppe of a Jagdgeschwader, although in some cases a Staffel within each Gruppe might be allotted the fighter bomber role. The advantage lay in the aircraft's speed and two methods of attack were employed. One was to approach above 20,000 feet then dive on the target and escape at low level, the other was to make a low-level dash across the Channel, climb sharply to altitude, bomb, then retreat at low level. Interception of such aircraft, which rarely operated above

Schwarm strength, was difficult, but on the other hand they caused little damage apart from nuisance and tying up quantities of defending fighters. When it came time to count the cost of the July to November air battles over England, the Luftwaffe Jagdgruppen found that 610 Bf 109s and 235 Bf 110s had been the price of a costly lesson, which had also accounted for 888 other German aircraft. Against this the RAF had lost 915 machines and 415 pilots. In the straight fighter versus fighter combats the Bf 109s had accounted for a total of 491 Spitfires and Hurricanes which in fact gave the German fighter a slight edge as far as total victories were concerned. Both sides had lost many experienced pilots who would be difficult to replace, among these being 22-year-old Major Helmut Wick, one of only three pilots to have been awarded the Oak Leaves to the Knight's Cross, who was shot down on November 28 while leading JG 2; at this time Wick had 56 victories to his credit.

By mid-November the assault against England lay in the hands of the night bombers, the day fighters being withdrawn to re-equip and rest. The failure of the Bf 110 in the heavy fighter role over England played a major part in it being assigned other roles including night interdiction, fighter bomber, and its most successful, night fighting, in which it became the mainstay of the Nachtjagdgruppen by the end of the war. Some Zerstörer units kept their Bf 110s for use in the day fighter role, but these were not seen again in English air space.

By early 1941 RAF Fighter Command had a strength of 1,467 aircraft in 76 squadrons and was now ready to strike back at those Luftwaffe units left in France.

In September 1940 I/NJG 2 started to operate against Bomber Command airfields in East Anglia using their Ju 88s to stalk returning bombers then attack them in the circuit as they prepared to land. At this time the crew were beginning to relax and drop their vigilance so there was always a good chance that the Luftwaffe intruder could make a successful fast pass at a landing bomber.

Although such operations did not achieve a very high success rate they continued until October 1941 when I/NJG 2 was moved to the Mediterranean. In the summer of 1943 Me 410s operating with the fifth Gruppe of KG 2 restarted intruder operations over British bomber bases, but by this time the Mosquito was fully operational and although the German twin proved an adequate adversary it was never able to operate with the equanimity so essential for this type of operation. None the less, intruders created a feeling of insecurity among bomber crews, and they could not be ignored. It was essential therefore to keep a certain number of defending fighters at hand to counter such operations and, while they were doing this, they could not interfere with the then sporadic efforts of the Luftwaffe night bombers.

The forerunner of the Me 410 was the 210 which it was hoped would be an ideal replacement for the Bf 110, but early operations proved that the hopes were ill-founded and although the aircraft started to equip two squadrons in 1941 it never achieved the success hoped for. In September 1942 the Me 210 made its operational debut over the British Isles when, on the sixth of the month, two were intercepted by Typhoons of No 1 Squadron and despatched into the sea.

After the hectic days of 1940 day fighters were rarely seen over England except, perhaps, when they chased short-of-fuel Spitfires back across the Channel, acted as fighter bombers, or escorted the latter on nuisance raids which became a feature of the fighter air war from then until 1944.

One of the most successful aircraft employed on this type of operation was the Focke-Wulf FW 190 which, when it made its debut over France in 1941, caused Fighter Command many problems. A first-rate fighter able to take a lot of punishment, the FW 190 was a natural for the low-level intruder role and it was not long before it was seen in varying quantities attacking coastal targets and eventually London.

As early as March 1942 Hugo Sperrle had ordered JG 2 and JG 26 to form Jagdbomber or Jabo Staffeln within each Geschwader for the sole purpose of attacking British targets. The two Staffeln formed were initially equipped with Bf 109F–4 models but these soon gave way to FW 190A–4s, which proved far more effective. As well as harrying shipping the two fighter Geschwadern in France were always looking for stray RAF fighters and, on the evening of June 23 1942, 7/JG 2 found such targets when they encountered Spitfires of the Exeter-based Polish wing returning from a strike against French airfields. During the ensuing combat the adjutant of III/JG 2 shot down a Spitfire then became disorientated and landed his FW 190A–3 at RAF Pembrey. Thus Oberleutnant

Arnim Faber handed to the RAF an intact aircraft for evaluation purposes, which enabled Fighter Command to at least appreciate the quality of fighter they were now facing.

Raids by fighters against RAF airfields brought back the days of 1940 but they were only shadows of the earlier efforts and in no way aimed at putting RAF fighter out of action for good; a task which was now well beyond the capabilities of the Luftwaffe. This type of operation tied up a tremendous number of RAF aircraft, personnel and ground equipment, and the results achieved by what amounts to only a few Staffeln from two Geschwadern were out of all proportion to the minimum effort required. The only way to combat either fighter or fighter/bomber raids was to mount standing patrols and these were often only able to intercept the intruders on their exit across the Channel. A typical example of such raids was the one mounted on October 31 1942 when FW 190s made an attack on Canterbury; approaching at low level the raiders were across the coast before Spitfires based at Hawkinge could be scrambled, the cathedral city was attacked and damage, as well as casualties, inflicted before the defending fighters, by this time with height advantage, despatched two of the now bombless fighter bombers into the Kent countryside and two more into the Channel. Efforts such as this, although not strictly speaking fighter operations, were carried out by fighter pilots who had not received any formal training in such tactics and learned as they progressed.

Until June 1944 the French-based Luftwaffe fighter units, which mainly comprised components of JG 2 and JG 26, put up a gallant struggle against increasingly superior numbers and equipment and, although they had little opportunity to operate in the pure fighter role over England, they fought as hard as their opposite numbers in the RAF had during the days of 1940 when the positions were virtually reversed. Throughout World War 2 the Luftwaffe fighter pilot earned the respect of his opponents in every theatre, none more than over England in 1940, when the cream of both air forces' fighter squadrons fought a battle the like of which will never be seen again, and in which many skilled pilots, who under different circumstances may well have been brothers-in-arms, paid the ultimate price. Such is the folly of war.

ABOUT THE PHOTOGRAPHS

The photographs in this book have been selected with care from the Bundesarchiv, Koblenz (the approximate German equivalent of the US National Archives or the British Public Records Office). Particular attention has been devoted to choosing photographs which will be fresh to the majority of readers, although it is inevitable that one or two may be familiar. Other than this, the author's prime concern has been to choose good-quality photographs which illustrate the type of detail that enthusiasts and modellers require. In certain instances quality has, to a degree, been sacrificed in order to include a particularly interesting photograph. For the most part, however, the quality speaks for itself.

The Bundesarchiv files hold some one million black and white negatives of Wehrmacht and Luftwaffe subjects, including 150,000 on the Kriegsmarine, some 20,000 glass negatives from the inter-war period and several hundred colour photographs. Sheer numbers is one of the problems which makes the compilation of a book such as this difficult. Other difficulties include the fact that, in the vast majority of cases, the negatives have not been printed so the researcher is forced to look through box after box of 35 mm contact strips – some 250 boxes containing an average of over 5,000 pictures each, plus folders containing a further 115,000 contact prints of the Waffen-SS; moreover, cataloguing and indexing the negatives is neither an easy nor a short task, with the result that, at the present time, Luftwaffe and Wehrmacht subjects as well as entirely separate theatres of operations are intermingled in the same files.

There is a simple explanation for this confusion. The Bundesarchiv photographs were taken by war correspondents attached to German military units, and the negatives were originally stored in the Reich Propaganda Ministry in Berlin. Towards the close of World War 2, all the photographs – then numbering some 3½ million – were ordered to be destroyed. One man in the Ministry, a Herr Evers, realised that they should be preserved for posterity and, acting entirely unofficially and on his own initiative, commandeered the first available suitable transport – two refrigerated fish trucks – loaded the negatives into them, and set out for safety. Unfortunately, one of the trucks disappeared en route and, to this day, nobody knows what happened to it. The remainder were captured by the Americans and shipped to Washington, where they remained for 20 years before the majority were returned to the government of West Germany. A large number, however, still reside in Washington. Thus the Bundesarchiv files are incomplete, with infuriating gaps for any researcher. Specifically, they end in the autumn of 1944, after Arnhem, and thus record none of the drama of the closing months of the war.

The photographs are currently housed in a modern office block in Koblenz, overlooking the River Mosel. The priceless negatives are stored in the basement, and there are strict security checks on anyone seeking admission to the Bildarchiv (Photo Archive). Regrettably, and the author has been asked to stress this point, the archives are *only open to bona fide authors and publishers, and prints can only be supplied for reproduction in a book or magazine.* They CANNOT be supplied to private collectors or enthusiasts for personal use, so *please* – don't write to the Bundesarchiv or the publishers of this book asking for copy prints, because they cannot be provided. The well-equipped photo laboratory at the Bundesarchiv is only capable of handling some 80 to 100 prints per day because each is printed individually under strictly controlled conditions – another reason for the fine quality of the photographs but also a contributory factor in the above legislation.

THE
PHOTOGRAPHS

Left The presence of welding equipment looks a little ominous for this Bf 109E-4 of JG 53. The camouflage netting and cover over the wing cannon and propeller blade are interesting (345/788/11A).

Above The spiral spinner markings were one of the Luftwaffe fighter pilots' favourite decorations and enhance the nose of this pre-war C-2 which carries the badge of JG 21 which later was used by JG 54 (318/53/6A).

Below This Bf 109B-1, identifiable as such by the scoop on the cowling forward of the cockpit, is an example of the first version to equip the Luftwaffe in any number. By 1939 most of them had been relegated to second-line duties, and it is likely that this one came to grief in the hands of a pilot under training (40/490/4).

Above The emblem of 2/JG 71 later II/JG 51 Mölders, is a familiar sight on Bf 109s, in this case it adorns a D-1. The refuelling point and windscreen make interesting comparison with the next photograph (337/11/14).

Left The later style windscreen and repositioned refuelling point can be clearly seen on this Bf 109E of an unknown Gruppen Adjutant. Note how the chevron is painted over the yellow fuel rating triangle (342/638/11).

Above Bf 109E-1s had the style of windscreen and canopy framing seen in this picture, but it was also used on some early production E-3s. The pilot listening to the Luftwaffe version of 'There I was upside down . . .', is an Unteroffizier and his pilot's badge can be clearly seen on his left side (426/389/38A).

Right The G-6 refuelling point was still in the same position as the E but now a loop aerial has been added aft of the normal communications aerial. Once again the individual markings encroach on the rating triangle (487/3066/34).

Left Mechanics wearing the familiar all-black overall carry out final checks on this Bf 109E-1 whilst two Unteroffiziers help a Leutnant into his parachute. He is wearing a one-piece flying suit which is normally associated with Luftwaffe bomber pilots and crews; the absence of a life-jacket could also indicate that he does not intend to venture too near the sea on this particular patrol (378/24/16A).

Below The pilot-type parachute very similar to those worn by RAF fighter pilots, forms the cushion on which this Bf 109E-1 pilot will sit during the forthcoming combat patrol (378/24/17A).

Right This Luftwaffe Hauptmann wears an Iron Cross first class on his left pocket, a second class ribbon on his tunic and a Knights Cross at his throat. He has no flying badge or insignia (343/653/18A).

Far right Officers' style hat badge and collar patches of this Hauptmann make interesting comparison with the rather ordinary buttons on the greatcoat (344/741B/24).

Below right The correct alignment and fire pattern of the wing- and fuselage-mounted armament was important and this board on the firing butts was used to check the sighting (381/104/24A).

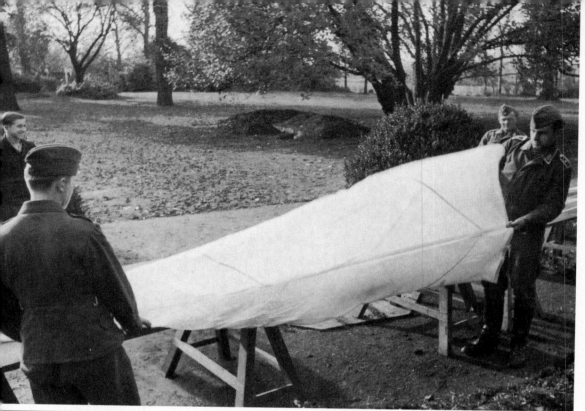

Above An essential part of any pilots' equipment is his parachute. On the right a Feldwebel opens the canopy to inspect the material . . . **left** the panels are folded neatly in order . . . **above right** the lines hooked into their correct places in the pack . . . **right** and the rip-cord release pins secure, the pack folded (345/773/12A, 22A, 25A and 36A).

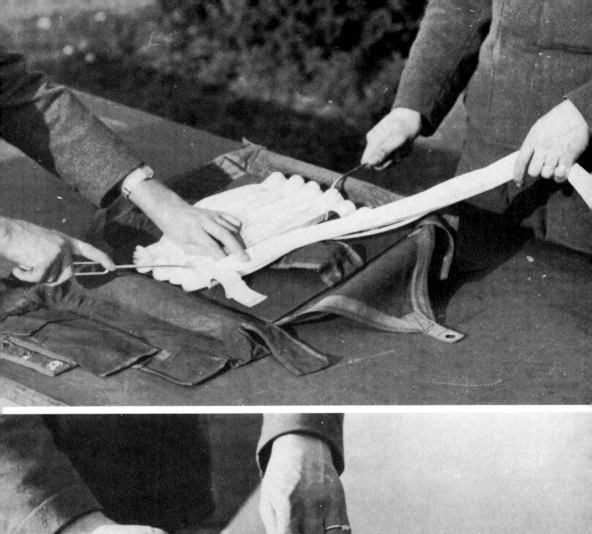

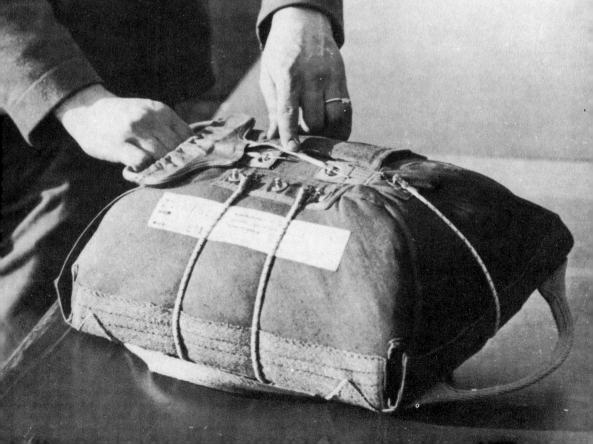

Above Naval personnel often flew as observers with the Luftwaffe and there are many instances recorded in the Battle of Britain of combined crews operating reconnaissance aircraft. These two Luftwaffe Leutnants seem pleased with their hands in this informal card school. A good diorama for figure modellers? (339/15/27).

Below Very early wartime flying kit is worn by these two pilots who appear to have mixed feelings about the canine world. The left hand figure is a Oberfeldwebel and his colleague is a Feldwebel (380/52B/27).

Above the interrupter gear of the fuselage-mounted MG17s being checked on a Bf 109E-1. The mechanic on the wing is slowly cranking the engine by hand and the large disc on the propeller enables him and his colleague to ensure that the cut-out circuits are functioning correctly. The wing ports for the wing-mounted MG 17s can also be seen and the drooped leading edge slots provide another noteworthy feature (381/104/14A).

Below Interrupter gear set, the MG 17s can now be checked and harmonised (381/104/6).

Above left These Bf 109E-3s have the camouflage normally associated with the Battle of Britain period, with Hellblau sides to the fuselage. The variation in demarcation is clearly evident between the two aircraft. The nearest machine is that of the Gruppe Adjutant of I Gruppe and has the Old Boot badge associated with I/JG 77, which was part of Luftflotte 5 in Norway, on its cowling (341/490/16A).

Left Airfield defence was in the hands of Luftwaffe ground gunners seen here bringing their 20 mm gun to readiness during a practice stand-to (382/215/32A).

Above The later windscreen and canopy of the E-3 is evident in this view of a Geschwader 1A (Operations Officer) aircraft (345/789/29A).

Above right The port wing cannon of a Bf 109E-3 which is probably from an early production batch as it has the windscreen and canopy framing associated with the E-1 (340/174/18A).

Right Revi gun sight, panel fixing, sliding window in canopy, and stylised name, all make useful contributions to this close up of the E-3 depicted in the above photograph (340/174/17A).

Background photograph The white cliffs of Dover seen from France. So close but yet so far as many a Luftwaffe fighter pilot, low on fuel, was to find out to his cost in the summer of 1940 (343/653/15A).

Insets above and above left Lingering too long over England or becoming too involved in a dog-fight could result in a long ride in a rubber dinghy, or a short, wet walk up the beach, as the pilots of these two Bf 109E-4s found when they underestimated their fuel consumption or combat duration (344/741/29 and 227/290/18).

Above Lowered flaps, aileron mass balances, and general wear to the paintwork, contribute to make this a very interesting picture. The aircraft is an E-4 of JG 26, whose Gothic 'S' badge on a white shield can be seen below the windscreen (345/797/33).

Below The bent propeller blades of this Bf 109E-4 photographed on December 23 1940, indicate that it has recently carried out a wheels-up landing. The aircraft belongs to 2/JG 26 whose badge on the cowling is similar to that of 9/JG 54 (345/797/32).

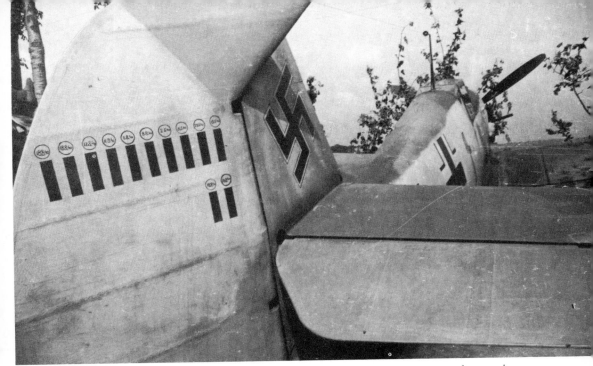

Above The 12 kill markings on the rudder of this Bf 109E-3 span a period of three months, starting on May 19 1940 and ending with four kills on August 18 (342/629/18A).

Below Typical kill markings being painted on a Bf 109E-3 of the 9th Staffel of III/JG 26 at Caffiers, August 1940. The Staffel badge is below the cockpit and the code and Gruppe markings are in yellow outlined in black. It is interesting to note that the splinter camouflage seen on the tailplane does not have a solid demarcation line (342/629/20).

Above An Unteroffizier (left) and Flieger examine the 56 kill markings on the rudder of a Bf 109E-4 of JG 26 flown by Adolf Galland (345/797/36).

Left The rudder actuating rod, tailwheel and general 'scruffy' appearance of the paintwork of this JG 26 Bf 109E–4 are all useful modelling details (345/767/38).

Above right This Bf 109D-1 carries the Hunter and Blunderbuss badge used at various times by I/JG 231, I/JGR 102 and I/ZG 2, all pre-war units, although ZG 2 operated Bf 110s during the Battle of Britain. The black hand on a white background in a red circle was later used by 8/JG 27. The early-style exhaust stubs and wing refuelling point are of interest (379/37/24A).

Right Victor and vanquished. Bf 109E-1 of JG 53 (Pik As) stands in front of what are possibly the remains of a Belgian Air Force Fairey Fox. The all-black Swastika and its position over the rudder hinge line are of interest (341/488/27A).

Left This Bf 109E-1, Wrk No 3489, belongs to JG 77 which was part of Generaloberst Hans-Jürgen Stumpff's Norwegian based Luftflotte 5 during the Battle of Britain (321/855/32A).

Below left The famous Ace of Spades badge of JG 53 on the nose of Staffelkapitän Hubert Kroeck's Bf 109E-1 in November 1939 (337/36/3A).

This page and the following five pages The ensuing are typical unit and personal badges seen on Bf 109s during early 1940:

Right Detail of the Cow badge for those who want to have a go at hand painting (340/175/13A).

Below Happy looking cow on Bf 109E-1 of JG 53—note mirror on windscreen (340/175/10A).

Above Personal markings on a Bf 109E-1 of JG 77 (321/855/28A).

Left Heraldic lion, possibly on Rudolf Lochner's Bf 109E-1 (340/174/20A).

Above right Another Bf 109E-1 of JG 53 with a Feldwebel on the cockpit edge (340/175/8A).

Right Personal emblem of an unknown pilot of JG 53 (340/175/18A).

Above left Apart from the badge, this also shows the windscreen, gun sight and exhaust system to advantage (340/174/14A).

Above and right A badge which could owe a lot to *origami* on the fuselage of a Bf 109E-1 of JG 53 (340/174/16A and 340/174/18A).

Left Gliders featured a great deal in training and sport flying in the Luftwaffe both before and after its existence was announced to the world. This Grunau carries a version of the famous 'Edelweiss' badge associated with KG 51, but it was at the time the photograph was taken with a Bf 109 unit, JG 53 (340/181/38A).

Above and left This pilot's mascot seems to be taking a great deal of interest in the Woodpecker badge which, in this case, is inscribed I Gruppe JG 71 in the top left and right hand corners. The badge was later used by JG 51 in a variety of colours and styles, some with the legend, some without. II/JG 51 aircraft sometimes carried it behind the fuselage cross as shown in the bottom picture. The umbrella is a 'dig' at Neville Chamberlain, the British Prime Minister at the outbreak of war. The legend 'Gott Strafe England' translates as 'God Punish England' (340/181/29A), (340/181/32A).

Above right A variety of camouflage styles can be seen on these Bf 109Es of II/JG 53. The aircraft in the foreground has its Swastika across the hinge line, whereas the second machine has it on the fin which was to become common practice during 1940 (341/479/17A).

Right There is a wealth of useful information in the photograph of an early Bf 109, probably a C-2, of I/JG 21. The badge is of the 3rd Staffel but this was later used by 9/JG 54. The metal pennant on the radio mast indicates the Staffelkapitän's aircraft. The officer with the map is an Oberleutnant (318/53/7A).

Left This Bf 109C-2 shows to advantage the early style spinner and deep radiator, the former being retained on the E model which equipped most Jagdgeschwadern operating over England in 1940, but the latter becoming less evident as the nose contours were 'cleaned-up' (594/292/18).

Below A II/JG 53 pilot recounts a recent combat success to other pilots as mechanics already move in on his Bf 109E-4 (345/789/36A).

Right This is an aircraft of II/JG 54 painted in camouflage usually associated with the Eastern Front. Once again there is much useful detail especially for the diorama enthusiast (346/849/28A).

Below right Some published works on Luftwaffe camouflage are quite dogmatic that the demarcation between colours on splinter camouflage was a hard line. This photograph of 9/JG 26 Bf 109Es taken in France, August 1940, proves this is not so. The *Hollen-Hund* badge of the 9th Staffel is in red and can also be seen on the Mercedes Benz 230 (Kfz 12) Field Car (342/629/25).

Above Useful close-up of Bf 109E-4 cockpit showing windscreen detail and Revi C12C gun sight (428/482/16A).

Below This group of JG 53 pilots with Hauptmann Bretnuk on the left are wearing their inflatable life-jackets over standard issue flight jackets. The piping on the two left hand figures' hats indicates officer rank (345/789/18A).

Above This officer of JG 26 is wearing a leather flight jacket, inflatable life-jacket and Luger. The JG 26 badge shows just one of the many styles used by this unit (426/383/35A).

Below Hauptmann Bretnuk of JG 53 with his mechanics in France, August 1940. The tail in the background belongs to a Ju 88 (345/789/30A).

Above left Galland taxis his Bf 109E-4 to dispersal after an operation on August 23 1940 (345/797/27).

Left A group of groundcrew personnel watch Galland's Bf 109E-4 as it moves towards its dispersal, possibly at Audembert in the Pas de Calais, during the summer of 1940 (345/755/26).

Above The Bf 109E was superseded in service by the F model which caused the RAF some problems in early 1941. This F-2 is the aircraft flown by Josef (Pips) Priller who served with JG 26 and 51 and ended the war with 101 victories. Priller is the figure nearest the fin and rudder (597/505/2).

Right Adolf Galland in the cockpit of his JG 26 Bf 109E-4. The Mickey Mouse emblem is the pilot's personal marking. This is a very familiar photograph but there is rarely any comment made about the unusual attachment to the gun sight which protrudes through the screen (345/755/28).

Background photograph Many of these Bf 110 crews listening to II Gruppe commander Hauptmann Ralph von Rettburg at Crécy in the summer of 1940, were to die in the skies over England as their aircraft proved an inadequate match for the RAF fighters (342/632/7).

Inset The Revi reflector gun sight, rearview mirror and canopy operating handle, are all part of the pilot's cockpit of a Bf 110 (382/216/25A).

Above Wreckage of another Bf 109E which failed to make its base on July 20 1940 and crashed at Cap Blanc (78/67/18A).

Left and right Hauptmann Hermann Joppien of JG 51 showing typical flight gear worn by officers during 1940 (346/803/31 and 26A).

Above An NCO pilot, in this case an Unteroffizier, of JG 26 discusses something amusing with a mechanic: could it be 'Where's my propeller!'? (345/797/35).

Far left Arguably one of the Luftwaffe's most famous aces, Walter Nowotny with JG 51 in 1940. He was killed on November 8 1944 whilst flying a Me 262 as commander of JG 7, at which time he had achieved 258 victories (464/6770/13).

Left Oberstleutnant ~~Heinz Joachim Huth,~~ the commander of ZG 26, a Bf 110 unit whose headquarters were at Lille during the Battle of Britain (342/632/22). *KESSELRING ?*

Below left The unmistakable figure of Generalmajor Adolf Galland, with the familiar cigar clamped between his lips, and three other members of JG 26 (343/653/39A).

Right A JG 53 pilot and his mascot in France, 1940 (345/788/7A).

Below Generalmajor Josef Priller (left) in discussion with a Leutnant whose cuff band shows him to be a member of JG 26 (342/628/20).

Above The propeller and spinner make a poignant guardian over the last resting place of Leutnant Erwin Michele who was killed on July 20 1940 (344/719/14A).

Right The white uniform, and portly figure make any caption unnecessary! (540/476/10).

Below Bf 109E-1 of I/JG 76 which became II/JG 54 in July 1940. Both pilots are NCOs, Feldwebels, as indicated by the rank badges of their one-piece flying suits, which were not often worn by fighter pilots after 1939 (380/52B/25A).

Above Armourers load the guns of a Bf 109E-1. The breeches of the twin fuselage-mounted weapons can be clearly seen just forward of the windscreen (321/855A/4).

Below Crews of ZG 26's Bf 110s being briefed before a sortie. They are wearing one-piece light brown flying suits with inflatable life-jackets (343/699/35A).

Above Useful undercarriage detail in this shot of an SC 250 bomb being loaded on to a Bf 109E-4/B (345/758/28).

Below Fighters were turned into bombers and ground support aircraft by the addition of bomb racks on wings and under the fuselage. This Bf 109E-4/B of II (Schlacht) LG 2 is having an SC 250 bomb loaded on to its centre-line rack (345/758/32A).

Above Engine installation, undercarriage and wing root detail of a Bf 109E (344/740/12).

Left Armourers fit an ammunition drum for the wing mounted cannon on a Bf 109E-4 (426/389/23A).

Above right The assembly hall for Bf 109s at the Messerschmitt works photographed in 1944. The aircraft are all G variants (680/8258/11).

Right This Bf 109F operated on the Eastern Front, but the picture shows how the cowlings and canopy were hinged (389/1072/30).

Left When the FW 190 came on the scene in 1941 it immediately gave the Luftwaffe an advantage over the RAF, but it was not without its teething troubles. II/JG 26 tested the aircraft under simulated combat conditions at Le Bourget, and overheating of the power plant resulting in total seizure of the engine was one of the problems encountered. This FW 190A-0 of II/JG 26 has just been sprayed with foam following an occurrence of this problem at Le Bourget (405/1711/31).

Below left An E-4 with hastily applied mottle on the fuselage, but of more interest is the open panel in the canopy roof, a feature not often seen or appreciated by the average enthusiast (342/628/7).

Right All you need to know about the flight gear of a Bf 110 pilot in 1940 can be found from this pleasing shot of a ZG 26 pilot (342/632/18).

Below Mess tins, it seems, were as vital to the German armed forces as they were to the British. These Luftwaffe mechanics take a break from work in France, 1940. The centre figure is a Feldwebel (Sergeant) and to his left is a Unteroffizier (Corporal) (343/697/20).

Left A JG 26 pilot poses beside Spitfire K9961 of No 64 Squadron. It is likely that he is the man responsible for shooting it down (342/628/14).

Below This Spitfire Mk 1a (K9961) was from the first production batch and was in the hands of a No 64 Squadron pilot when it came to grief in France in June 1940 (342/628/12).

Right and below right Swordfish L9724 was taken on charge at 24 MU on June 30 1938 and formed part of HMS *Glorious'* strike element. When the carrier was engaged in ferrying fighters to Norway, the Swordfish operated from shore bases. It is thought that this particular aircraft was shot down during night operations in the Dunkirk area in May 1940 (345/793/27A and 23A).

OVERLEAF

Background photograph The
FW 190A-3 of the operations
officer (Ia) Hauptmann Wilhelm
Gäth, of JG 26 is pushed back
into its shelter during 1942
(604/1527/10A).

Left inset Like the Bf 109 the
FW 190 was also used as a nuisance raider and for ground support duty. This A5/U8 has a 550
lb bomb on its centre-line rack
and is about to set out from its
base in France to make a low-
level assault on an English target
(623/3003/20).

Right inset This rather pleasing
air-to-air shot of an FW 190A-5
is believed to be that of Pips Priller and taken just prior to the
1944 invasion when JG 26 rep-
resented the only fighter unit
available to give support over
the invasion beaches
(298/1753/6).

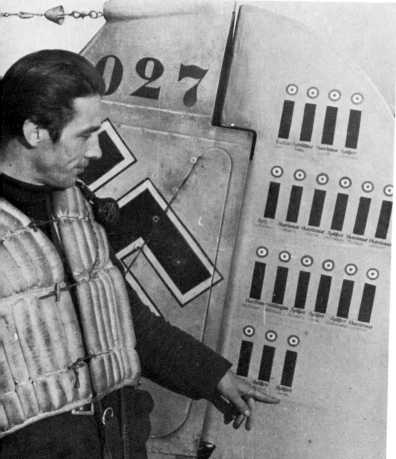

Above The poor forward vision from the cockpit is well illustrated in this view of a JG 2 FW 190A-3. The 13 is yellow-edged in black and camouflage is 74/75/76 (226/197/37).

Left The kill markings on the rudder of this FW 190A-3, believed to be of JG 2, show eight Hurricanes, nine Spitfires, a lone Wellington and a Curtiss. Scenes of victory range from France for the Curtiss, to London for one of the Hurricanes (226/197/7).

Above right The clean and functional lines of the big radial-engined fighter can be appreciated in this view of an FW 190A-3 with a service test unit (367/2398/13A).

Right The fate of the Queen is forgotten as two pilots of the 8th Staffel of II/JG 2 are called to scramble their FW 190A-3s. The stylised bird emblem was developed from the exhaust stains which marred all FW 190's fuselage paintwork aft of the cowling (619/2686/14A).

Above left Luftwaffe personnel take a close look at the opposition in the form of Spitfire Vb SD-E: AA837 of No 501 County of Gloucester Auxiliary Air Force Squadron (226/168/11A).

Left An already loaded F-8 makes an appropriate back-drop for an armourer carrying out final adjustments to a 500 kg bomb's detonator (464/381/11).

Above A Feldwebel supervises the loading of a 500 kg bomb on a French landing strip in 1944 (496/3493/5A).

Above right The FW 190G-8/R5 could carry bombs under its wings as well as the fuselage as shown by this typical installation on a II/JG 1 aircraft in 1944 (500/102/37).

Right These FW 190G-8/R13s have two 66 Imperial gallon wing tanks and a 500 kg bomb on their fuselage rack. The pilot is wearing a back-type parachute but has not yet adjusted the leg straps of the harness (496/3493/25).

Background photograph A Bf 110C-3 of 5/ZG 26 creates a miniature dust storm as its starts its take-off run at Crécy in 1940 (343/668/14).

Left inset It is interesting to conjecture what thoughts are going through the mind of this ZG 26 pilot as he surveys the sky from the wing of his Bf 110 (342/630/10A).

Below left inset These two Bf 110Cs of ZG 26 (*Horst Wessel*) carry two entirely different camouflage patterns (342/632/14).

Below inset A 5th Staffel Bf 110 of ZG 26 with three kill markings on its rudder, taxis out at Crécy in 1940 for another sortie over England (342/630/12A).

Above left Fire would seem to be mainly responsible for stripping the fabric from this Hurricane's fuselage, but no doubt Luftwaffe souvenir hunters also had a hand in it (382/227/5).

Centre left This Fairey Battle, L5231, was powered by a Merlin 3 and belonged to the AASF. It carries the code of No 142 Squadron (QT) which it has been alleged was only carried on the unit's Wellingtons. This aircraft is believed to have been shot down whilst attacking the Meuse bridges in 1940 (341/466/22A).

Below left This Spitfire II is a presentation aircraft, the legend below the windscreen stating 'Daily Telegraph' with the name 'The Shopmate' in script below. It was operated by No 611 Squadron West Lancashire Auxiliary Air Force (226/176/3).

Above This Spitfire N3290 was a Mk 1a and (**above right**) this Hurricane BE221 was a Mk IIB, before they met their respective ends from the guns of the Luftwaffe (342/645/2A and 226/155/24).

Right This Blenheim IV, T2036, was one of a batch built by Rootes securities and finished by the Luftwaffe in France during 1940 (344/741/6).

Above left This air-to-air shot of a Bf 110C-1 of I/ZG 76 shows the clean lines of the aircraft and is worth comparison with the seemingly cluttered outline of the later G series which were most successful as night fighters (382/211/32).

Left The Luftwaffe hoped for a lot from the twin-engined heavy fighter units equipped with the Bf 110, but they proved to be outclassed by RAF fighters and eventually had to operate with their own fighter escort. This example is a C-1 of I/ZG 76 (379/7/5A).

Above All the plumbing and armament of this FW 190A-8 is revealed as mechanics and armourers work on the 14-cylinder twin row BMW engine behind which can be seen the twin fuselage-mounted MG 131s (676/7960/19A).

Right The Ia officer of a II Gruppe is helped into his parachute harness (353/1642/22).

Left Gunner and pilot board a Bf 110C-1 of ZG 76. The fuselage insulation point for the aerial, loop aerial, first-aid location point and retractable step, are all useful modelling details (321/855A/14).

Below left A candid shot of an FW 190A-5/U8 with practically all cowlings open as well as small inspection panels (under wings) seemingly ready to invite inspection (375/2706/13A).

Right An FW 190A-4 of III/JG 2 is readied for its next sortie. The position of the first-aid equipment is marked with a small red cross just forward and below the fuselage marking (604/1543/13).

Below This officer is wearing the cuff band of JG 2 and the rank badges of Generalmajor. His glasses are no doubt lined up on Dover's white cliffs, which made popular viewing by this method in 1940 (343/680/3A).

Background photograph This FW 190A-5/U8 carries unusual markings, especially the one aft of the chevron. This has only been seen on a handful of FW 190 photographs, all of which have been fighter bombers, and accurate and authenticated information would be most welcome (628/3482/4).

Left inset The famous Dragon badge of ZG 52 which was formed in 1939, on the nose of one of the unit's Bf 110C-1s (341/455/11A).

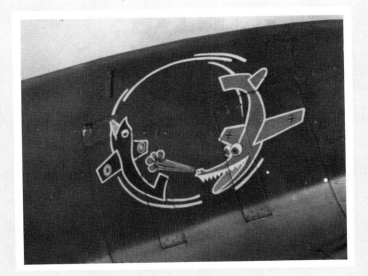

Right inset *Der Ringelpitz* marking on the nose of a I/ZG 26 (*Horst Wessel*) Bf 110. A red painted German alligator chases a black British fish; both open mouths are red (399/11/24).

Above The RAF had an expression '26 on the tail' when help was required to push an aircraft, no doubt something similar was used in the Luftwaffe, but in the case of this Bf 110 it would seem to have also included the engines (339/114/14A).

Right Hay bales bring the work to within reach for these mechanics working on a Bf 110D of III/ZG 26 (343/668/13).

Below Fuel is taken on board this C-3 as mechanics and possibly the pilot and gunner take a lot of interest in the port engine (382/215/21A).

Above Five kill markings indicate a new 'ace' for 5/ZG 26 in France 1940. The two-tone green splinter camouflage on rudders contradicts some statements that most Bf 110s of this period were in one shade of green only (342/632/17).

Below This is the business end of the Bf 110C-3 seen in the above photograph (342/632/9).

Above This 2nd Staffel aircraft of I/ZG 76 has its Swastika painted across the rudder hinge line (339/114/13A).

Below This one of an unknown unit, has it just on the fin. The dog and armed guard could indicate that the second photograph was taken in occupied territory (600/1133/213).

Above The amount of contribution from the two pushing on the intake under the port wing must be open to some question! Aircraft is from the 5th Staffel of ZG 26 and is in typical camouflage of the 1940 period (343/699/37A).

Below The famous Clog emblem of II/ZG 26 can be seen alongside the Ace of Spades marking of the 5th Staffel on this Bf 110C-3 (343/668/9).

Above It seems to be rest and relaxation time for at least some of the ground crew of II/ZG 26, or are they just posing for the man with the cine camera? Diorama enthusiasts should find plenty of scope with the hay bales and camouflaged netting (343/699/14A).

Below Hay bales form the walls of an improvised shelter for this Bf 110C-3 of 5/ZG 26. The Staffel emblem is usually associated with JG 53 (Pik As), but was a popular marking in the Luftwaffe and also appeared on No 81 Squadron RAF P-47s in the Far East (342/630/9A).

Above Crews of 2/ZG 76 being briefed by a Hauptmann before a sortie over England in 1940 (379/12/21).

Right The sea was neutral. Both sides mounted air sea rescue operations for downed flyers since recovery of a trained pilot more than compensated for the loss of an aircraft. In this case it looks as though the He 59B is too late in coming to the aid of this German airman (343/469/16A).

Below A Feldwebel holds back the canopy hatch whilst the gunner of this Bf 110C-4 boards. The MG 15 is in the stowed position and the aircraft's Werke number—1369—is painted on one of the canopy panels. How many modellers using the large scale Bf 110 kits available have included that detail? (339/114/7A).

Background photograph This Bf 110C-3 M8 + DP of 6/ZG 76 carries the Shark's mouth decoration which resulted in this Gruppe becoming known as the Haifisch Gruppe (382/211/11).

Left inset Many of the present day arguments regarding colour schemes and finishes could be solved by a stroll along this line of Bf 110s of II/ZG 76. Exhaust stains and weathering along the undercarriage doors of the nearest aircraft are interesting (382/211/22).

Below inset A useful close-up of the Shark's mouth marking and port engine cowling of a Bf 110C of ZG 76 (382/212/39).

Above Two styles of helmet, standard issue Luftwaffe goggles, and the familiar one-piece flying suit are of interest, but of greater interest is the Oberleutnant on the right, who is wearing a tinted monocle over his left eye! (382/216/27A).

Left The camera stops the action as a ZG 76 crewman dons his parachute. Once again the two-tone green splinter camouflage is very evident on the Bf 110C (379/12/26).

Above right A Major and a Hauptmann take a lot of interest in the refuelling of a Bf 110C-1. Note the badly stained wing and stencil marking on the flap (379/2/24A).

Above far right The officer on the right is an Oberleutnant and he wears the flying badge of a pilot on his right pocket. The wearing of spectacles seems a little odd especially as close examination shows them not be sun glasses (382/215/29A).

Right Nine aircraft victories starting on May 15 1940 and ending on September 11, and three balloons destroyed all on June 11, decorate the starboard rudder of a Bf 110 of ZG 26 (343/697/27).

Left and below Bf 110s suffered badly at the hands of Hurricanes and Spitfires. Quite often those which returned to their bases were badly damaged or had wounded crewmen on board. These two photographs show a wounded gunner being removed from a Bf 110C of ZG 26 (343/699/24A and 343/699/25A).

Right A Bf 110C-3 of 2/ZG 76 photographed in late 1939. The individual letter D is in red outlined in white and the Swastika has been painted across both the fin and rudder (379/7/3A).

Below right Block and tackle being used to raise a new port engine into its mounts on a Bf 110C-1 of 3/ZG 76. Note the control lock on the starboard rudder (379/3/17A).

Above A Hauptmann helps one of ZG 76 groundcrew add camouflage to a Bf 110C. Note the picket point behind the aircraft's tail wheel and cover over the canopy (379/12B/13).

Below Loading the four MG 17 7.9 mm machine-guns in the nose of a 2/ZG 76 Bf 110C-1 (379/7/18A).

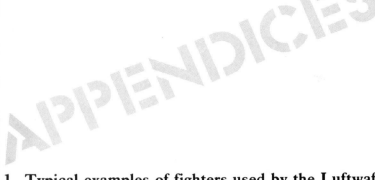

1. Typical examples of fighters used by the Luftwaffe over England

Messerschmitt Bf 109E–4

Span:	32 feet 4½ inches. Length: 28 feet 8 inches.
Engine:	Daimler Benz DB 601A 12-cylinder, liquid-cooled.
Performance:	Maximum speed 345 mph at 12,300 feet, 245 mph at 16,400 feet, service ceriling 36,000 feet.
Armament:	Two 7·9 mm MG 17 machine-guns with 1,000 rpg firing through propeller arc, and two 20 mm MG FF cannon, with 60 rpg, in wings.

Messerschmitt Bf 110C–4

Span:	53 feet 4¾ inches. Length: 39 feet 8½ inches.
Engines:	Two Daimler Benz DB 601A 12-cylinder, liquid-cooled.
Performance:	Maximum speed 349 mph at 22,960 feet, service ceiling 32,000 feet.
Armament:	Four 7·9 mm MG 17 machine-guns with 1,000 rpg and two 20 mm MG FF cannon with 180 rpg. One rear-firing 7·9 mm MG 15 machine-gun with 750 rpg in rear cockpit.

Focke Wulf FW 190A–4

Span:	34 feet 5½ inches. Length: 29 feet.
Engine:	One BMW 801D–2 with MW 50 supplementary fuel injection.
Performance:	Maximum speed 416 mph at 20,600 feet, service ceiling 37,400 feet.
Armament:	Two 13 mm MG 131 machine-guns and four 20 mm MG 151 cannon (could vary).

---

2. Fighter units as at August 1940

Luftflotte 2

Jagdfliegerführer 2 All with three Gruppen unless otherwise stated.
JG 3 – All Gruppen equipped with Bf 109E
JG 26 – All Gruppen equipped with Bf 109E
JG 51 – All Gruppen equipped with Bf 109E
JG 52 – Two Gruppen only, both equipped with Bf 109E
JG 54 – All Gruppen equipped with Bf 109E
I Gruppe Lehrgeschwader 2 – Bf 109E
ZG 26 – All Gruppen equipped with Bf 109E
ZG 76 – II and III Gruppen only, both with Bf 110

Luftflotte 3

3 Staffel Aufklärungsgruppe 31 – Bf 110

V (ZG) Lehrgeschwader 1 – Bf 110
2 Staffel Aufklärungsgruppe II – Bf 110
Jagdfliegerführer 3
JG 2 – All Gruppen with Bf 109E
JG 27 – All Gruppen with Bf 109E
JG 53 – All Gruppen with Bf 109E
ZG 2 – I and II Gruppen with Bf 110

Luftflotte 5

I Gruppe ZG 76 – Bf 110
JG 77 II Gruppe – Bf 109E
Aufklärungsgruppe 22 – Bf 110C

3. Fighter and fighter bomber units in the west as at May 1942

Jagdfliegerführer 2

JG 26   Stab, I, II, III gruppe – FW 190A–3, 10
(Jabo) Staffel – Bf 109F–4/B

Jagdfliegerführer 3

JG 2   Stab, Stabschwarm, I Gruppe Stab and 3 Staffel – Bf 109G–2, 1 and 2 Staffeln – Bf 109G–2, II Gruppe, III Gruppe – FW 190A–3, 10 (Jabo) Staffel – Bf 109F–4/B

4. Fighter and fighter bomber units in the west as at May 1943

JG 2   Stab, I and II Gruppen – Bf 109G–2 and G–6, III Gruppe – FW 190A–4

JG 26   Stab and III Gruppe – FW 190A–4, I Gruppe detached to Eastern Front, II Gruppe – FW 190A–4 and A–5

JG 27   1 and 2 Staffeln – Bf 109G–6

JG 54   11 Staffel – Bf 109G–6

SKG 10   Stab, I, II and IV Gruppen – FW 190A–4/U8, III Gruppe in Mediterranean Theatre

Other titles in the same series

No 1 Panzers in the Desert
by Bruce Quarrie

No 2 German Bombers over England
by Bryan Philpott

No 3 Waffen-SS in Russia
by Bruce Quarrie

No 4 Fighters Defending the Reich
by Bryan Philpott

No 5 Panzers in North-West Europe
by Bruce Quarrie

No 6 German Fighters over the Med
by Bryan Philpott

No 7 German Paratroops in the Med
by Bruce Quarrie

No 8 German Bombers over Russia
by Bryan Philpott

No 9 Panzers in Russia 1941–43
by Bruce Quarrie

In preparation

No 11 U-Boats in the Atlantic
by Paul Beaver

No 12 Panzers in Russia 1943-45
by Bruce Quarrie

No 13 German Bombers over the Med
by Bryan Philpott

No 14 German Capital Ships
by Paul Beaver

No 15 German Mountain Troops
by Bruce Quarrie

No 16 German Fighters over Russia
by Bryan Philpott

No 17 E-Boats and Coastal Craft
by Paul Beaver

No 18 German Maritime Aircraft
by Bryan Philpott

No 19 Panzers in the Balkans and Italy
by Bruce Quarrie

No 20 German Destroyers and Escorts
by Paul Beaver